The C TALKING T·r·o·u·s·e·r·s

TESSA KRAILING

Illustrated by Jan Lewis

PACIFIC
L E A R N I N G

© 2001 Pacific Learning
© 1999 Written by **Tessa Krailing**
Illustrated by **Jan Lewis**
US Edit by **Alison Auch**

All rights reserved. No part of this publication may
be reproduced or transmitted in any form or by
any means, electronic or mechanical, including
photocopying, recording, taping, or any information
storage and retrieval system, without permission in
writing from the publisher.

This Americanized Edition of *The Case of the Talking
Trousers,* originally published in English in 1999, is
published by arrangement with Oxford University
Press.

05 04 03 02 01
10 9 8 7 6 5 4 3 2 1

Published by
Pacific Learning
P.O. Box 2723
Huntington Beach, CA 92647-0723
www.pacificlearning.com

ISBN: 1-59055-038-2
PL-7407

Contents

1
Beagle and Co.

This story is about a club called Beagle
and Co. Beagle's full name is Daniel
Beagle. He even looks a little like a dog,
with floppy hair and a long nose. It's
just the right size, his mom says, for
sniffing out trouble. His best friend is
Jamal, sometimes known as Jam.

Jamal is a math wizard. He carries around a calculator and is always figuring stuff out with it.

He's even calculated that his grumpy next-door-neighbor, Mr. Briggs, loses his temper over one thousand times a year. That's three times a day.

No wonder Mr. Briggs has such a red face all the time!

Marietta is the third member of the club. The rest of the club sometimes try to leave her behind, but mostly they let her come along because she's very good at figuring things out. Not math, like Jamal, but mysteries.

The fourth member of the club is Wesley Clark.

Poor Wesley was born unlucky. There was the time he went to meet Beagle and Jamal down by the river and heard a voice calling from an empty bench...

2
Hello? Hello?

Wesley finished his lunch. He looked at his watch. It said 1:58.

"Oh, no!" he groaned. He'd promised to meet Beagle and Jamal down by the river at 2:00 P.M. Now he was going to be late. Would Beagle and Jamal go to the baseball game without him?

He hurried out of the house and ran all the way to the river.

No sign of Beagle and Jamal.
Wesley looked at his watch again.
To his surprise it said 1:47.

"Oh, no!" he groaned. When he looked at it before it must have said 1:38, not 1:58! Now, instead of being late, he was early. He flopped down on an empty bench to wait.

Wesley looked around. All he could see was a pair of gray trousers lying on the bench beside him. They looked as if they had been carelessly tossed there by someone in a hurry, but there was no sign of their owner.

"Hello? Hello? Are you still there?"

Wesley stared at the trousers. No, they couldn't be...

"Hello? Hello?" bellowed the voice.

They were! The trousers were talking to him!

"Um, hello," said Wesley, nervously.

"Ah, there you are!" said the trousers.

"I didn't go anywhere," said Wesley.

"Huh? What did you say?"

Reluctantly Wesley moved a little bit closer.

"I'm sorry, but I've never talked to a pair of trousers before."

"Oh, never mind," said the voice crossly. "Can you take me to the station, please?"

Wesley hesitated.

He wished that Beagle and Jamal were here, but he was alone by the river – with a pair of talking trousers!

"Hurry up!" snapped the trousers. "I have a train to catch. Can you take me or not?"

"Well, yes... I guess I could," said Wesley doubtfully.

"Huh? Did you say yes?"

"Yes!" shouted Wesley.

"Okay, then, please hurry up." There was a click.

Wesley stood up. He stared at the trousers. "Are you sure you want to go to the train station?"

The trousers said nothing. They seemed to be sulking.

Nervously, Wesley picked them up. They felt heavier than he expected, but then these were no ordinary trousers. They were talking trousers.

Wesley sighed. Why did this sort of thing always happen to him? Reluctantly, he carried the trousers toward the train station.

3

Help! Help!

Beagle and Jamal arrived at the river. "Wesley's not here," said Beagle. "I bet he's late."

Jamal looked at his watch. "How long should we wait? We don't want to miss the beginning of the game."

"Let's give him five minutes, okay?" said Beagle.

They stood by the river, waiting.

Suddenly, a small black-and-white dog appeared beside them. It shook itself hard, spraying water everywhere.

"Where did that dog come from?" asked Beagle.

"I don't know," said Jamal. "It wasn't there a minute ago."

Beagle stared at the dog. "It's wet."

"It must have been swimming in the river," said Jamal.

They looked back up the path, hoping to see Wesley, but there was still no sign of him.

"Come on, Jam," said Beagle. "We've waited long enough."

They turned to go.

"Help!" called a voice.

HELP!

They stopped and looked around, but there was no one there except the dog. They turned away.

"Oh, please help me!" called the voice. "This water's freezing!"

Jamal pointed. "Look – there's someone in the river!"

A man's face appeared in the cattails.

At that moment, someone else whistled and the dog ran off along the riverbank.

"Humph!" said the man. "So that's all the thanks I get for rescuing their pesky little dog!"

Beagle went closer.

You rescued the dog?

"Yes, I did!" The man brushed the water out of his eyes.

"I was sitting on that bench, eating my lunch, when I saw the dog fall in the water. It seemed to be in trouble, so I dived in to rescue it."

"That was brave of you," said Jamal, admiringly.

"I didn't stop to think." The man shivered.

"You'd better get out of the water or you'll catch a cold," said Beagle.

"I can't," said the man. "Someone has stolen my trousers."

"Stolen your trousers?" said Beagle and Jamal together.

"I took them off before I dived into the water. I'm sure I left them on that bench, but they seem to have disappeared." The man shivered again.

"Why would anyone want to steal your trousers?" asked Jamal.

"For money, I guess," said the man. "There was some loose change in the pocket. Also my car keys. I don't suppose I'll ever get them back now." He looked cold and miserable.

Beagle felt sorry for him. "What can we do?" he asked.

"Find me some dry clothes," said the man. "I can't get out of the river in just my shirt and boxers."

Beagle and Jamal exchanged looks. They each knew what the other was thinking. Where could they find him some dry clothes? It might take a long time. Did this mean they'd have to miss the baseball game?

Still, they couldn't leave the man in the water, could they?

Beagle sighed. "Don't worry," he told the man. "We'll find you something to wear. Come on, Jam."

4

The Trousers Aren't Talking

Marietta was on her way to the Girl Scouts' rummage sale. Halfway down Station Road she met Wesley carrying a pair of trousers.

"Hi, Wesley," she said. "I thought you were going to the game with Beagle and Jamal."

"I was," Wesley said sadly, "but now I've got to take these trousers to the train station."

Marietta stared at the trousers.

Whose are they?

"I don't know," said Wesley. "I found them down by the river when I was waiting for Beagle and Jamal."

"Why are you taking them to the train station?" asked Marietta.

"Because they asked me to," said Wesley. "They told me they had a train to catch."

Marietta laughed.

Wesley turned red. "I'm not kidding. These trousers can talk!"

He looked so serious that Marietta stopped laughing. "Okay, then," she said, "ask them a question."

Wesley looked down at the trousers.

Um, where do you want to go?

No answer. The trousers were silent.

Marietta sighed. "Oh, Wesley! Why don't you give them to me? I'm taking this stuff to the Girl Scouts' rummage sale." She showed him the bag she was carrying.

Wesley looked shocked. "These trousers aren't junk! They're special. Besides, I promised to take them to the train station."

Marietta started to laugh again. "All right – you'd better hurry or they'll miss their train," she said. "Bye, Wesley!"

Still laughing, she continued on her way toward the rummage sale.

At the end of Oak Street, she met Beagle and Jamal.

"Are you looking for Wesley?" she asked. "Because if you are, I just saw him. You'll never guess what he..."

"Sorry, we can't stop," said Beagle.
"We're in a hurry."

"But this is funny," said Marietta.

"What's in there?" interrupted Beagle,
pointing at the bag she was carrying.

"Old stuff," said Marietta, surprised.

"What kind of old stuff?" he
demanded. "Any old clothes?"

"Yes, lots," said Marietta. "Sweaters,
jeans – stuff my brother and I grew
out of."

Beagle looked disappointed. "Kids' stuff. That's no good. Anything for grown-ups?"

Marietta opened the bag and looked inside. "Only an old bathrobe..."

Beagle looked thrilled. "Can we have it, please?"

She stared at him, amazed. "Why? What do you want it for?"

"We met a man..." said Jamal.

"Down by the river..." said Beagle.

"He jumped into the river to rescue a dog..." said Jamal.

"Someone stole his trousers," said Beagle. "He's furious about it and wants to catch the thief. So we promised to find him some dry clothes."

Jamal nodded. "That's why we need the bathrobe."

It'll cover him up.

"We-ell," said Marietta doubtfully. "Mom gave it to me specifically for the rummage sale..."

"This is much more important than a rummage sale," said Beagle. "Please, Marietta – give us the bathrobe."

Reluctantly, she took it out of the bag. It was pink and fluffy and made of terrycloth.

"Oh," said Beagle, disappointed. "It's a woman's bathrobe."

"It was my mom's," said Marietta.

Don't you want it?

"Yes, we'll take it." Beagle practically grabbed it out of her hands. "Come on, Jamal, let's go."

Puzzled, Marietta watched them go down the street. They were acting almost as strangely as Wesley with his talking trousers...

Trousers?

Down by the river?

Were the trousers Wesley had found the same trousers Beagle and Jamal said were stolen? They hadn't said anything about the trousers being able to talk. What a mystery!

Marietta decided not to go to the rummage sale after all. Rummage sales were boring. Talking trousers were definitely more interesting.

She turned and ran back toward the train station to look for Wesley.

5

Pink and Fluffy

Beagle and Jamal went back to the river. "Good news!" Beagle called out. "We found something for you to wear."

The man's face appeared in the cattails. "That was quick!"

"We met a friend going to a rummage sale," said Jamal. "She gave us this bathrobe."

The man stared at it. "But – but – but it's pink! And fluffy!"

"It belonged to our friend's mom," said Beagle, "but it will cover you up."

"It's made of terrycloth so it'll also dry you," Jamal said.

I guess it'll have to do.

The man climbed out of the river and put on the bathrobe.

He looked down at his bare feet. "Do you see my shoes anywhere? I took them off before I dived into the river."

Beagle searched the ground around the bench. "Here's one!" he called, pulling a big black shoe out of the grass.

"Here's the other one!" said Jamal. They carried them over to the man.

"Huh! Lucky the trouser thief didn't steal those too." He put them on.

They looked very odd with the fluffy pink bathrobe.

"Did you happen to notice if my cab is still parked at the end of the road?" said the man.

"Your cab?" said Beagle.

The man nodded. "My taxi. I left it there when I came down to the river to eat my lunch. If it's gone I – well, just wait until I catch that thief!"

"I did see a cab parked at the end of the road," said Jamal. "It has a sign on the door that says 'Frank's Taxis'."

The man looked a little happier. "That's mine all right. I'm Frank."

"I'm Beagle," said Beagle.

"Thanks, Beagle. Thanks, Jamal," said Frank. "You've both been a huge help. Now, I'd better get back to my cab and start chasing that thief."

He started off along the path with the fluffy pink bathrobe flapping around his bare legs.

"We'll come with you," said Beagle.

They found the cab, and then Frank groaned.

"Oh, no! I forgot – the trouser thief took my car keys!"

"What will you do?" said Beagle.

"I'm going to call the police," said Frank. "The sooner they catch that villain, the better."

"How are you going to call them?" Beagle asked. "You can't get into your cab without the keys."

"No, I'll use my – " Frank stopped.

"Use your what?" Beagle asked.

"Oh, no!" Frank groaned again. "That was in my pocket too!"

"What was?" asked Jamal.

Frank didn't answer. He was already striding up the road.

"Frank? Frank, where are you going?" Beagle called after him.

"Over to the police station," Frank called back.

Beagle and Jamal looked at each other. "Do you think the police will believe him?" Beagle said.

"Not in that bathrobe," said Jamal. "Come on, we'd better go with him."

6

The Trousers Have a Train to Catch

The train station was crowded. Marietta couldn't see Wesley anywhere. She looked in the ticket office. No Wesley. She looked in the coffee shop.
No Wesley. She even looked in the lost-and-found. No Wesley.

Marietta was stumped. Where could he be?

Then she saw a sign saying "Station Manager's Office." Maybe she should ask in there.

The door was open a crack. She could hear voices inside – a man's deep voice and a boy's.

Wesley!

Marietta rushed inside.

The station manager sat behind his desk. Wesley stood in front of it, still clutching the trousers. They both turned to stare at her.

"Hi, Wesley," she said.

I've been looking for you everywhere.

The station manager looked stern. "Do you know this young man?"

"Yes, his name is Wesley Clark," said Marietta. "I need to talk to him... right now."

"Talk to him about what?" asked the station manager.

Marietta hesitated. "About those trousers…"

"Ha!" said the station manager. "The famous talking trousers, which – this young man says – told him to take them to the train station!"

Marietta looked at Wesley. She noticed that his ears were bright red.

"So," the station manager went on, "he took the trousers to the ticket office and asked them where they wanted to go. Surprise, surprise! – they refused to answer him."

Wesley's ears turned purple.

"Soon," said the station manager, "there was a long line behind him. A line of passengers wanting to buy a ticket. After a while they got tired of waiting – and that's when they sent for me!"

"It's not my fault," Wesley muttered. "I have no idea why the trousers have stopped talking... Who knows – maybe they fell asleep."

"Ha!" exploded the station manager. "I've heard some strange stories in my time, but this one beats them all."

"I don't know about the trousers being able to talk," said Marietta, "but I think I know who they belong to. Did you say you found them by the river, Wesley?"

Wesley nodded. "I went there to meet Beagle and Jamal, but I got there too early. Then I heard these trousers calling to me. They were lying on a bench..."

"That's because a man had jumped in the river to rescue a dog," said Marietta. "Beagle and Jamal met the man afterward, and he told them someone had stolen his trousers."

"Stolen?" said the station manager.

I knew it!

Wesley looked nervous. "I didn't mean to steal them. I was only doing what the trousers told me to do..."

"Oh, forget about what the trousers said," said Marietta. "We've got to find Beagle and Jamal so they can give the trousers back to their owner. Come on!"

"Not so fast, young lady!" The station manager rose from his chair. "If these trousers have been stolen, I think I should call the police."

Wesley looked even more nervous.

"Please don't do that," said Marietta. "You heard what Wesley said. He didn't mean to steal them. It was a mistake."

"A mistake?" The station manager shook his head. "I'm not so sure about that. However, you seem like a sensible young lady – "

"I am," said Marietta firmly. "I'm a very sensible young lady."

"In that case…"

The station manager stopped.

"All right," he said, "I'll let you both go. But I'm keeping the trousers."

Wesley clutched them tighter than ever. "They've got a train to catch!"

"Put them down on that chair,"
commanded the station manager.
"When you find their owner you can
bring him back here to get them."

"You'd better do as he says, Wesley,"
said Marietta.

Very reluctantly, Wesley put the
trousers down on the chair.

Marietta went to the door. "Come
on, let's go find Beagle and Jamal."

7

Wesley Tells the Truth

Beagle, Jamal, and Frank had just
reached the steps of the police station.
To their surprise they saw Marietta
racing toward them.

"It's all right," she called out. "I found
the stolen trousers. You don't need to
tell the police."

They all turned to stare at her.

"Did you say that you've found my trousers?" asked Frank.

"Yes, they're at the train station," said Marietta. She giggled. "You look kind of funny in my mom's old bathrobe!"

"Okay, okay," said Frank, "but how did my trousers get to the train station?"

"Wesley took them there," said Marietta.

"Wesley?" exclaimed Beagle and Jamal together.

Then Beagle noticed that Marietta was not alone. Wesley stood half-hidden behind her. "Is it true?" he asked. "Did you take Frank's pants?" Wesley nodded.

It was a mistake.

"He didn't mean to steal them," Marietta said to Frank. "Unfortunately the station manager thinks he did, so he's keeping the trousers until you pick them up."

"At least someone's got some sense!" said Frank. He set off up the street toward the train station.

"We'd better go with him," said Beagle. "You too, Wesley. You're the one who started all this."

Reluctantly, Wesley followed.

Marietta took them to the station manager's office. Frank knocked on the door.

"Come in!" boomed a deep voice.

Frank poked his head around the door. "I believe you've got my trousers?" he said.

"Well, I've got *somebody's* trousers," said the station manager. "You'd better come inside."

They all trooped into his office. He stared at Frank's fluffy pink bathrobe.

"Ah, there they are!" said Frank. He picked up the trousers from the chair.

"Just one moment, sir," said the station manager. "May I ask how you came to lose your trousers?"

"He took them off before he jumped into the river," said Beagle.

"To rescue a dog," said Jamal.

"Wesley found them on the bench," said Marietta.

The station manager looked hard at Wesley. "This young man told me," he said, "that the trousers asked him to bring them to the station."

Everyone turned to stare at Wesley.

Wesley's ears turned red again. "It's true!" he muttered. "They said they had a train to catch."

"Oh, Wesley!" said Beagle.

Everyone burst out laughing. Everyone except Frank.

"Wesley's not crazy," he said. "He's telling the truth."

Frank put his hand into one of the trouser pockets and pulled out – a cellular phone!

"I was answering a call when I saw the dog in the water," Frank explained. "A man was calling for a taxi ride. He'd told me his address but not where he wanted to go. I must have put the phone back in my pocket before I took my trousers off..."

"So that's what Wesley heard!" exclaimed Marietta. "A man saying he wanted to go to the train station."

Wesley looked a little happier. "He did sound annoyed," he said.

"I'm not surprised," said Frank. "He's probably still waiting. I'd better go right away."

He gave Marietta back her mom's old bathrobe and put on his trousers.

"In that case, sir," said the station manager, "do you still wish to charge this young man with theft?"

"Of course not," said Frank. "It was a mistake anyone could have made. Good-bye, kids."

After the kids left the train station, Beagle said, "Frank was being nice. I don't think just anyone could have made that mistake. Only Wesley."

The others agreed.

Even Wesley.

When Jamal got home his mom said, "Our neighbor Mr. Briggs lost his temper again today. He called for a cab to take him to the train station, but it didn't come. He was furious!"

Jamal laughed. He couldn't wait to tell Beagle and Co.

About the Author

I wrote my first story
when I was four years
old. I always knew I
wanted to be a writer,
but it was many years
before my first book
(which was about
dinosaurs) was published.
Since then I have written over thirty
books for children of all ages. Best of all,
I like writing mystery stories.

I usually start by asking myself the
question, "What if…?" For example, what
if Wesley was walking along the river when
he found a pair of trousers? What if the
trousers started to speak to him? What a
mystery!

Tessa Krailing